The Only Thing Cheap is the Seat

A love letter to the great game of baseball, featuring anecdotes, advice and analysis to entertain and educate casual fans and true fanatics alike.

Brian D. Eyre

The Only Thing Cheap is the Seat

A Love Letter to the Great Game of Baseball

Copyright © 2013 Brian D. Eyre

All rights reserved.

Cover Photo: "Honey, I'm Home"
Copyright © 2010 Brian D. Eyre

ISBN: 978-0615764313

DEDICATION

For Kim, Margaret, Jana and Lance. Thanks for reminding me that the love of baseball is not only about advanced metrics and cold beer. It is also about family, friendship, community, simplicity and, of course, The Cheap Seats.

CONTENTS

A Love Affair 1

Good Seats are Still Available 5

Tailgating and Batting Practice 10

Hey Mister! Can I Get an Autograph?........... 18

Don't Keep Your Eye on the Ball 27

Listen to the Umpire...................................... 36

Who's on First?.. 42

Let's Take a Break... 46

Don't Be That Dude 51

The Fine Art of Heckling 60

Seat Surfing... 65

Baseball Reindeer Games............................ 76

That Doesn't Make Sense 82

Second Guessing Second Guessers............ 94

Money Bull.. 102

Advanced Metrics in Quotes........................ 108

The Walk Off... 118

A Love Affair

"I see great things in baseball. It's our game - the American game."

— Walt Whitman

Brian D. Eyre

I fell in love with the game of baseball before I'd ever seen a game. I didn't even have a home team when I fell in love with the game of baseball. I was born near Dallas, Texas in the early sixties. The Dallas Cowboys were my introduction to the concept of sports. Back then, the Cowboys weren't called America's Team, they were called Next Year's Champions.

I was too young to know what that meant then. I probably thought it was a good thing. Both of my parents rooted for the Cowboys even though they were from Ohio and grew up as fans of the Cleveland teams. When I was about six years old, I came to realize that the Cowboys' rival was the Redskins, so I decided to root against the Redskins no matter who they were playing.

When my mother noticed me doing that, she told me that it's almost never right to root against a team. She told me to just root for my teams. I asked her when it would be right, and she said only if it's the despicable New York Yankees of Major League Baseball.

By the time I was seven, I was checking the box scores in the paper every day to see if the Cleveland Indians had won the night before. I was also checking on the Yankees. Those incredibly few occasions when the Indians won and the Yankees lost were great days for me.

At eight, I was collecting baseball cards and reading every box score of every game. I knew who played every position for every team in Major League Baseball. I knew who was playing well and who was in a slump. I would have dominated my second grade fantasy baseball league if there had been such a thing back then.

I mention all that to get to this point. When I learned that the Washington Senators were moving to North Texas to become the Texas Rangers, it was a better day for me than every Christmas and birthday I had ever enjoyed….. combined.

Brian D. Eyre

The purpose of this book is not to share my life story, although I suspect that might make an interesting book. My goal here is to share the great game with other fans and help make the game more enjoyable for everybody.

In almost fifty years as a baseball fan, I've learned some things about the great game that should interest even the most casual fan. I've also learned some things that might surprise the most intense fan.

Good Seats are Still Available

"Good Seats, Hey Buddy?"
— Beer Company Advertising Slogan

Brian D. Eyre

If I had a dollar for every time I've heard the phrase, "Good seats are still available," I'd be a wealthy man. It's a phrase that's used in every promotional campaign for every event ever promoted. Good seats are still available for political rallies, motivational speeches, music concerts and comedy performances.

Good seats are also still available, according to the promos for sporting events such as baseball games. Those seats, of course, are the subject of this book. A typical baseball stadium has about 40,000 seats. A ticket can cost anywhere from three dollars to several thousand dollars, depending on what game you attend, where you sit, and where you buy the ticket.

But, at least in baseball, good seats are always available. The question is, what constitutes a good seat at a baseball game. For a fanatical baseball fan like me, every seat to a baseball game, including a chair in my living room or a stool at a sports bar is a good seat.

But I'm not writing this book for me, I'm writing it for you. If you've decided to be a baseball fan, or are thinking about going to a game to see if you might be a baseball fan, you need to know what a good seat is. I can't answer that question for you, but I can help you answer it for yourself.

Seat selection is mostly subjective, but there are a few secrets to selecting seats that are helpful for the casual fan, as well as the season ticket buyer. I present the:

Seven Secrets of Seat Selection

1. If you attend the game to visit or chat with friends who are going with you, do not sit in the lower infield section unless your seat is behind a protective net.
2. If you attend the game to get drunk and prove you can be a loud and

offensive heckler, do not sit in the family section.

3. Regarding the previous secret, do not sit next to the family section either. Those fans are sitting there specifically because they do not want to be with you, being one aisle away doesn't help.

4. If you are scared of heights, don't sit in the upper deck, unless you've verified that you can sit there without having a panic attack. Many people who are scared of heights find that sitting in the upper deck isn't a problem, but getting to the upper deck on the escalator or the staircase is. If this is true for you, don't despair. Most stadiums have an elevator that goes to the upper deck. Even if it's a service elevator, an usher or other employee will usually allow you to

access it if you explain your issues to them.
5. If you aren't scared of heights, but you plan to drink alcohol during or before the game, don't sit near the front rows of any upper deck.
6. If the summer heat in your area bothers you, choose a seat that has either shade or a breeze, preferably both.
7. If you have a small bladder, or intend to consume copious amounts of alcohol during the game, choose a seat that is close to a restroom which is appropriate for your gender.

At the ballpark, every seat is a good seat for somebody, but if you take advantage of these secrets, you'll have a better chance of knowing that your seat is a good seat for you.

Tailgating and Batting Practice

"That's baseball, and it's my game. Y' know, you take your worries to the game, and you leave 'em there. You yell like crazy for your guys. It's good for your lungs, gives you a lift, and nobody calls the cops."

— Humphrey Bogart

The Only Thing Cheap is the Seat

Invariably, when I invite a friend to join me at a baseball game, the first question I'm asked is "What time do we need to leave?" My answer is always the same, "Whenever you want to leave."

The baseball game will begin at a certain scheduled time, but the gates generally open a couple hours before that time. The gates will also stay open well after the first pitch.

Being late to a baseball game can cause you to miss some of the fun, but it's not the end of the world. A baseball game consists of eighteen half-innings or seventeen if the home team leads. If you arrive in the middle of the third inning (30 to 45 minutes late), you only get to watch twelve or thirteen of them. Of course, if you happen to get lucky and catch an extra inning game, you get bonus half innings.

The thing is that baseball is a long season. When Major League Baseball releases its schedule, every team is down for 2,916 half-innings. Some half-innings never get played either because the home team doesn't need the last one or because of rain or other issues. Some innings end up being added, either because of extra innings or a game having to be added to the schedule to break a tie.

The point is that very few of even the most ardent fans actually watch every one of almost three thousand half-innings a season. And if you are one of those fans who must catch every inning, DVR technology makes it possible to record every game and see whatever you missed when you get home from the game.

Having said that, I don't mean to imply that you should want to be late. I'm simply stating that if you have to work or have other commitments that keep you from making the game for the opening pitch, you can still go to a game and have a great time. My preference is to get there early, because there's so much to do before the game ever starts.

Most people associate tailgating with football, but tailgating can be just as much fun at baseball games. The parking lots usually open several hours before the game, which gives you plenty of time to grill some hot dogs, have a cold beer or two, play catch with your family or friends, or engage in almost any other hobby.

Washers, bean bag toss, Nerf™ basketball, real basketball, television watching, and hacky sack are just a few examples of tailgating activities that can be enjoyed before a baseball game.

There are really only two rules that apply to tailgating. The first is that you need to remember that your tailgating/party place is also somebody else's parking lot. Make sure you leave room for others to drive their cars past your setup and room for others to park their cars, and make sure you don't crank your tunes so loud that nobody else can hear their own tunes or conversations.

The second is to keep it fun for everybody. As difficult as it may be to accept, not everybody roots for your favorite team. Good natured back and forth between fans of different teams only adds to the enjoyment of America's pastime.

Actual anger, hatred and vitriol do not. Nobody loves baseball, or their team, more than I do, but it is absolutely not worth fighting over. Trust me, as fans of the great game of baseball, Red Sox and Yankee fans have more in common with each other than they have in common with more than 90% of the world.

I recommend that you welcome the other team's fans to your ballpark by thanking them for spending their hard earned money contributing to your team's financial resources and future payroll. When attending games on the road, remember that you are a guest and behave appropriately.

Tailgating is only one of the activities that you can enjoy before the game. You may prefer to spend that time inside the ballpark. Before most games, both teams take batting practice, and this is open to the ticket holding public.

The batting practice schedule will vary by team, weather and game time, but if you go into the stands a couple hours before game time, you

The Only Thing Cheap is the Seat

should be able to catch at least some of it. Batting practice is always conducted with the batters at home plate surrounded by a metal cage and the pitcher on or near the mound behind a protective screen.

If you see these things in place when you get in the stands, chances are very good that batting practice is either happening or about to happen. When batting practice ends for both teams, the cages usually come down pretty quickly.

Batting practice is usually more of a warm up than a practice. Few players actually hone their hitting skills in batting practice. The pitching is mostly fastballs that aren't very fast so the batters can loosen up. While that makes it less of a practice, it can make it more fun to watch.

Many players become legendary for their awesome displays of power in batting practice. Some of those are superstars like Reggie Jackson and Barry Bonds, Others are guys who carved out marginal careers over the years, but could still provide a fantastic show during batting practice.

If your home team or the visiting team has one of those guys, you can try to find that out before the game and look for him. You might also find out who that guy is just by following the crowd. If a large group of people start crowding into batting practice at the same time, it may signify that one of those players is expected to hit soon.

For me, the batting practice display is more fun when it comes from an unexpected source, like the time I watched a young player hit five majestic home runs in a span of about eight swings. The fact that the player only lasted a couple of non-descript seasons did little to take away from that one display.

Some people prefer tailgating to entering the stadium and watching batting practice. Others prefer batting practice or just hanging out in the stadium enjoying the virtually free rein that comes with entering hours before the first pitch.

The Only Thing Cheap is the Seat

Personally, I enjoy both, and many ball parks accommodate both. At some parks, you can tailgate for a bit, go in to watch batting practice, and still go back out to tailgate.

If that's your plan, make sure you confirm that you can reenter before you go in. Also, make sure you're clear on where and how to get your ticket scanned out and/or validated as you exit, to make sure you can get back in.

Hey Mister! Can I Get an Autograph?

"Any ballplayer that don't sign autographs for little kids ain't an American."

— Rogers Hornsby

The Only Thing Cheap is the Seat

Pregame is also a time to get autographs from the players. Since Rogers Hornsby issued his statement about autographs, ballplayers and America, the autograph world has changed. What used to be a hobby for children has become a business for many adults. That said, I offer this guide for autograph seekers.

The first thing to realize is that the player does not owe you an autograph. No matter how long you stand in the sun and wait for him, he does not owe you the autograph. Sadly, this rule also applies to your lovable, cute, perfect child, even on said child's birthday.

Most players will sign autographs when they can; and lovable, cute children have a better chance to get an autograph than an adult male, who appears to the player like a guy who just wants to sell the autograph on eBay.

I repeat, though, the player does not owe anybody an autograph, particularly not prior to a game. Imagine if you were in your office preparing for a big sales presentation, and fifty kids were lined up in the hall between your office and the conference room holding pens and paper up for you to sign.

The first time it happened, you might be pleasantly surprised, and gladly sign each one until the absolute last second before you had to give the presentation. By the tenth time, it might seem less like an honor and more like an imposition. Now imagine having it happen almost 200 times a year for your entire career.

The good news is that many of the players never quit signing autographs, and try to accommodate as many fans as they possibly can. Once you understand that the player doesn't owe you an autograph, here's how to maximize your chance of getting one.

First, make sure you have something to be signed and a writing tool. The universal autograph tool is the medium Sharpie. It works great for baseballs, programs, and most other souvenirs. However if you want something signed that doesn't lend itself to being signed by

The Only Thing Cheap is the Seat

Sharpie, make sure you have the correct writing tool.

Once you have the tools, pick a location. If you're looking for a particular player, you need to pick it based on where he is likely to be. If, for instance, the player you want is a starting pitcher, don't even think about trying to get his autograph on the day of a game he is starting.

If the player is a position player, meaning any player other than a pitcher, you will need to hang out between home plate and your team's dugout. You should try to catch his attention as he finishes batting practice, not as he is preparing for batting practice.

Pitchers don't often take batting practice. They also have their own version of a dugout. The pitchers' 'dugout' is called a bullpen, and its location can vary from ballpark to ballpark. Some are behind the outfield fence, while others are down the base lines on the field of play.

If you're looking for a pitcher's autograph, your first step is to find the bullpen. The one thing all bullpens have in common is two pitching rubbers and two home plates 60' 6" apart where pitchers can warm up. If you have trouble locating the bullpen, ask an usher or other ballpark employee.

Relief pitchers and starting pitchers on their off days can sometimes be found in the bullpen or wandering around on the outfield warning track pretending to be shagging flies or doing calisthenics. Sometimes, signing an autograph or two out there is a good way to take a break without risking the manager's ire.

Obviously, if you see the player you want signing autographs, try to get in line. Remember, though, that the autograph line is not like the grocery store line. It doesn't always move in an orderly fashion that ensures that everybody gets what they want eventually. The autograph line can end without warning, and not everybody gets what they want.

My advice is to be polite, but insistent. If you are a drinking man or woman, think of it like the

The Only Thing Cheap is the Seat

bartender at last call. You have to try to get there, but if you make a jerk of yourself trying to get there, you know you may get kicked out empty handed.

Let's assume you make it, you've handed the baseball and the Sharpie to your favorite all time player. What happens next depends on many variables. If he's a superstar, who isn't worried about how much his autograph will be worth at card shows, he may just sign it quickly and hand it back to you.

If that's what you want, great, but if you really want it personalized for your wife or daughter, that won't work. If you want it personalized, ask for that before you hand over the ball or the Sharpie. (This can often get you signed quicker, because personalized souvenirs are worth far less on the open market and are never the goal of collectors).

If the player agrees to personalize it, don't ask for a long inscription, and definitely don't assume that the player will spell the name the way you expect. You need to say something along the lines of, "Mr. Ballgame, could you please dedicate this to my daughter Kathy?" Then hand him the Sharpie, "She spells it with a 'K,' K a t h y. Thank you."

The other thing to remember when looking for a certain player's autograph is that you really need to know the player in question. If you're not a big fan yourself or if you're getting the autograph for somebody else, you should buy a program to make sure you know who's who.

One of the saddest persons I ever met at a ballpark was the guy who told me he was waiting for the gates to open so he could get in and get the right autograph for his daughter who lived in another state with her mother. It seems that Pudge Rodriguez was her favorite player, and he'd previously gotten Alex Rodriguez' autograph by mistake.

Since I'm an optimist, and Pudge was one of the most fan and autograph friendly players in MLB history, I'd like to believe he achieved his goal. If nothing else, thanks to his experience, and my tendency to talk to strangers, I'm able to pass this lesson on to you.

Which leads us to the person that just wants an autograph from a player without caring which player or just wants as many autographs as possible. This is a more reachable objective, but it is not without its risks. The first is that when you specifically want 'Mr. Ballgame's' autograph, it's easier to sound authentic in your desire for his autograph.

The second is that not everybody on the field with a uniform and name and number on his (or her) back is one of the players, coaches or managers. Batboys, ballboys, bullpen catchers and occasionally friends of staff members wear uniforms just like the team members. I've personally witnessed a bullpen catcher laughing with one of the pitching coaches about the autographs he signed.

Now, it is possible that those autographs all went to members of the Bullpen Catchers Fan

Club of America, but I doubt it. A program will help you avoid that mistake. It will also help you get autographs from players you aren't familiar with by letting you know their names before you get close enough to ask for the autograph.

Don't Keep Your Eye on the Ball

"The vast majority of people who watch baseball can properly call 95% of all plays that happen on the field. My job is to teach you how to call the other 5%."

— Jim Evans

Brian D. Eyre

If you typically watch baseball on television, the first thing you'll notice when you attend a game is that there is no play by play in the stadium. You can bring your radio and listen in, but I don't recommend it.

Going to the game should not be an attempt to duplicate the experience of watching it on television. It should be its own experience.

However, many casual fans are used to relying on the announcers in order to know what is happening. Additionally, some fans aren't easily able to follow the game from the cheap seats, because their eyes aren't used to tracking the ball from that distance.

Also, even fans with great vision and expensive seats will often find themselves unable to see the ball for one reason or another. Almost every seat in every stadium has at least a few places on the field of play that are obstructed by something. Even the few that don't will eventually be obstructed by a fan or a ballpark employee.

The Only Thing Cheap is the Seat

I've never been to a game, nor talked to anybody who claims to have been to a game at which he or she was always able to see the ball. Personally, I don't believe it's even possible.

The good news is that the game can be enjoyed quite easily without seeing the ball, if you know what to watch. In many cases, it's even easier to tell what's happening if you don't watch the ball. One example of this is the routine fly ball to the outfield. If you've ever been to a game, you've heard the excited screams of the home crowd when a ball is hit to the outfield.

Of course, the screams slowly fade as the crowd gradually realizes its hero did not, in fact, hit a historic, majestic home run. I sometimes laugh when the crowd does this, but I probably shouldn't. The reality is that it's not easy to judge a fly ball. That's one reason not every fast athlete is a great outfielder.

It's even harder to judge a fly ball from various seats around the stadium, especially if you only sit in that seat a couple of times a year.

Also, getting excited is part of what makes baseball a fun game to watch. So, I suggest that you should be excited whenever you want, but I can also help you be one of the first to know if you have in fact witnessed a majestic home run.

The secret, as foreshadowed by the title of this chapter, is not to keep your eye on the ball. Yes, I realize little league coaches all over the world will cringe when they read this, but the fact is, you aren't trying to catch the ball, you're trying to catch the game. There's a huge difference.

I mentioned earlier that judging a fly ball is difficult, and it is, but one group of people can be expected to be very good at it. That group is headlined by Major League hitters, pitchers, outfielders and umpires. I list them in that order specifically because that is the order in which they can help you know where the ball will land.

I start with the hitter because at the point when the bat hits the ball, this is where most fans are looking. The hitter has spent most of his life learning the art of hitting a baseball. He will know, without fail, if he hit the ball well. Some hitters will also celebrate at the plate if they know they've hit a home run. This is also known as showing up the opposing pitcher, and is, as such, not popular with opposing pitchers. It also won't be popular with his teammates or manager if it turns out that the home run he was celebrating actually wasn't a home run.

Most hitters either have enough class not to show up the opposing pitcher or enough fear of looking like a fool to not celebrate at the plate. However, almost all hitters react differently when they crush a ball than on a normal hit. They will drop the bat slightly differently, start toward first base in a slightly more relaxed pace, or simply have a different sense of élan, after hitting a historic tape measure home run. If the hitter drops the bat, and sprints to first like normal, it may still be a home run, but it's almost certainly not a homerun that is likely to be the lead story on ESPN Sports Center, unless the game situation warrants the headline.

Depending on where you're sitting, you may be able to observe the pitcher and the hitter at the same time. Even if you can't, you can glance to the pitcher. His reaction can be just as helpful as the hitter. After all, he's spent most of his life learning to keep people from hitting his pitches. He usually knows when he has failed. In fact, he often knows before the batter even hits the ball.

The first thing you need to know about the pitcher's reaction is that if he points straight up in the air after the ball is hit, he believes the ball has been hit in the air, but not deep. This is because, and this might be amusing, sometimes the players on the field can't find the ball, either. By pointing up, he is letting the infielders know where he thinks it is. By happy coincidence, he also lets the fans know at the same time.

On the other hand, if the pitcher reacts with disgust when the ball is hit, he probably knows that the home run he just gave up is going to be on Sports Center. He may show disgust in a variety of ways: throwing down his glove or hat, turning his back to the plate, kicking or stomping at the mound or, my personal favorite, walking toward home plate with his glove out demanding a new ball from the umpire.

However, he does it, he's extremely likely to be right. Just like the hitter's teammates and managers won't like it if a batter stands at the plate admiring a home run that isn't a home run, the pitcher's manager and teammates won't like it if a pitcher stands at the mound having a fit instead of getting in position to back up the throw on a hit that turns out not to be a home run.

The outfielders are less emotionally invested in the question of is it or isn't it a massive home run, but they are much more practically involved. It is the outfielder's job to catch the ball if it is, in fact, not a home run. The outfielder has also spent most of his life learning to catch fly balls.

Most have also been catching fly balls long enough to know what effort it will take to catch one. If you think you see a massive home run, but then see an outfielder jogging back casually, you probably haven't. It is more likely that you're watching a fly out.

I say probably because it's possible that he has misjudged it or that he knows it's a homerun, but wants to show his manager that he's not a lollygagger. That possibility is quite remote, however, since very few outfielders at the Major League level are particularly likely to do either of these things.

Once you have this quick read on what is happening, it is usually confirmed quickly. Either the outfielder settles under the ball for an out or the hitter starts jogging around the bases to complete his home run. Occasionally, however, it isn't that simple. Sometimes your view of the outfielder is obstructed or the batter isn't sure what happened either and just keeps sprinting.

This is where the umpire can become your television broadcaster. No, he won't take a microphone and tell you what happened, but he will signal what happened. It is his job to make the call and to communicate that call.

The Only Thing Cheap is the Seat

The umpire may not have better eyes than all of the fans. He may not have a better point of view than all of the fans. He does, however, have both the right and the responsibility to make the call. What he sees, or thinks he sees, goes down in history as what happened.

Obviously, the previous paragraph is changing somewhat due to the advent of Instant replay review. However, unless review overturns become far more commonplace than they were at the time this tome was published, the rare overturns won't negate the point.

Since the umpire makes the call that counts and he communicates that call, he can be your source for information about any play you don't quite see either because of distance or obstructed view. All you have to know is how to listen to him. The next chapter will teach you how to do this.

Listen to the Umpire

"It isn't enough for an umpire merely to know what he's doing. He has to look as though he knows what he's doing too."

— Larry Goetz

The Only Thing Cheap is the Seat

Earlier, I mentioned that you sometimes need to 'listen' to the umpire. You won't necessarily be able to hear them, but if you're familiar with the hand signals that the umpires use, you can immediately 'hear' exactly what they are saying. Keep in mind that umpires are individuals, and some variance in the actual signal will occur.

Every time an umpire makes a call, it is supposed to be made verbally and physically. The story is told of an umpire at second base who simultaneously screamed "Safe!" and signaled out by holding his right hand in the air. Both the fielder and the runner looked at the umpire with puzzled looks.

The umpire looked at the runner sheepishly. "Well, my good man, the three of us heard me say that you're safe, but thirty thousand people saw me call you out. I'm afraid majority rules. You're out!" I doubt if that ever actually happened, but I've heard it told many times. The point is that from any seat in the stadium, you can hear the call.

There are four umpires, and it helps to know which one to look for, in what circumstance. Obviously, the home plate umpire, makes the calls on balls and strikes. Most umpires call a ball by simply not calling a strike. If the umpire makes no signal, it means the pitch is a ball. A very, very few umpires, almost none at the major league level will call balls by indicating where the pitch missed the strike zone.

A called (non-swinging) strike is indicated by raising the right hand. Many umpires have signature strike calls that may vary slightly from the basic right hand in the air, such as a fist pump, a boxer's punch or the like, but they all involve right hand movement, and are usually easily identifiable as such.

A swinging strike is also indicated with the right hand, usually by pointing at the batter or at the bat. In order to count as a swing the batter must be ruled to have gone around on the swing. Going around can be defined by any combination of the following admittedly unclear

The Only Thing Cheap is the Seat

phrases: crossing the hitting zone, committing to the swing, breaking his wrist, and countless other definitions which are no more helpful.

Given the ambiguity of the definition, it is no surprise that the home plate umpire is often unsure of what to call. In these cases, he may point at the umpire on the corner base to ask if the batter did, in fact go around on the swing. If he asks, and the batter did swing, the base umpire will raise his right hand to signal strike.

If he checked his swing in time, the base umpire will either spread his arms to signal safe, or make no call at all. Many umpires, will simply fold their arms as if disinterested to indicate that the batter didn't swing. This gesture is most common when the catcher initially requested the appeal (more on this in a later chapter).

All umpires are responsible for calling runners safe or out. An out, like a strike, is indicated with a raised right hand. Again, each umpire will have his own style, but if the right hand comes up, it means out. Safe is indicated by spreading both hands. It is important to note, especially at home plate, that safe doesn't simply mean 'not out.' Safe means the runner has reached the base (safe harbor).

On a close play at home plate, if the umpire doesn't signal safe or out, it means that the runner is not out, but has not touched the plate and is therefore, not safe.

The umpires also signal fair or foul, but that responsibility doesn't always fall to the same umpire. Which umpire is responsible for the call depends on where the ball is as it passes either first or third base.

If the ball is foul, and it's the plate umpire's call, he will raise both arms in the air to call time. If the ball is fair, the home plate umpire will either point toward fair territory or make no signal.

If it's the base umpire's call, he will first point toward foul territory, and then call time by raising both arms. If it's fair, he will simply point toward fair territory and the play will continue.

Don't worry about which umpire will make the call, because when the call is made, the other umpires will mimic it. Also, the players reactions will make it clear. If the ball is bouncing around in the left field corner and the batter is jogging back to home plate, that is a foul ball.

The base umpires are also responsible for calling home runs and safe or out on fly balls. The home run is called by raising the right hand and spinning the hand in a circle, It's unfortunate, but this signal is very similar to the signal for out, so if you lose sight of your potential home run and see the umpire raise his hand, don't give up until you make sure he is just signaling out, not home run.

Now that you can 'hear' the umpires' signals, you'll be able to 'see' every play no matter how obstructed your view becomes. Feel free to still get excited about home runs that turn out to be routine fly balls, if you wish.

Who's on First?

"I throw the ball to Who. Whoever it is drops the ball and the guy runs to second. Who picks up the ball and throws it to What. What throws it to I Don't Know. I Don't Know throws it back to Tomorrow, Triple play!"

— Bud Abbott (and many others)

The Only Thing Cheap is the Seat

One of the first people you'll likely see at the ball park is somebody hawking programs. The price varies from city to city, but generally a program is one of the less expensive souvenirs one can buy. It may also be the most useful. You don't have to buy a program to enjoy the game, but I recommend it to those wishing to enjoy the total ballpark experience.

Programs vary from stadium to stadium and from series to series, but every program I've ever seen contains certain elements that can be of value to any fan. Programs include a seating chart and a guide to concessions. The second is very valuable if you plan to buy food or beverages. The first is helpful if you plan to return to the ball park or if you might go seat surfing, as will be discussed in a later chapter.

As was discussed in an earlier chapter, programs can be invaluable in the search for autographs, if that's your thing, because that's where you can learn about the players whose autographs you might wish to seek.

Another thing that you can find in the program is a scorecard. Only the most ardent fans ever actually kept score at a ballpark, and almost nobody does it any more. However, the scorecard does include some basic information that can be helpful in one's attempt to understand what is happening on the field.

For the purpose of keeping score, every fielder has been assigned a number corresponding to his defensive position. These numbers are also used on the scoreboard to assign credit or blame to a particular player.

These numbers are as follows:

1	Pitcher
2	Catcher
3	First Baseman
4	Second Baseman
5	Third Baseman
6	Shortstop
7	Left Fielder
8	Center Fielder
9	Right Fielder

The Only Thing Cheap is the Seat

Thus, if you see a ground ball hit to the third baseman who throws to the second baseman who doesn't catch it, you don't have to wonder who messed up. The scoreboard will either post "E5" if the error is on the third baseman for a bad throw, or "E4" if the error is on the second baseman for not catching it.

Programs also have stories about the team and its players and off-field personnel that make for fascinating reading either during the game or days, weeks or years later. I did not set out to write this book to try to encourage program sales, but I do think it's possible that the program is the best value to be had at the ball park other than the seat.

Let's Take a Break

"A hot dog at the ballpark is better than roast beef at the Ritz."

— Humphrey Bogart

The Only Thing Cheap is the Seat

Baseball is a wonderful game, but it is only one of the many things one can enjoy at the baseball park. If you paid hundreds of dollars to sit in the front row, you probably will want to spend as much time as possible enjoying the view from your valuable real estate.

If, however, you wisely invested in a ticket in the cheap seats, you might want to enjoy some of the other amenities the ball park has to offer. As an added benefit to sitting in the cheap seats, you may also have some money left to spend.

As you read this chapter, please recall that the title of this book is *The Only Thing Cheap is the Seat.* Other than watching the game, or watching people at the game, almost everything else there is to do at the ballpark is most definitely not cheap.

The previous chapter covered the value of the program. Other than the program, the first obvious choice for spending that money is on something to eat and drink. The ballpark hot dog that Humphrey Bogart recommended is still a popular option, but it is by no means the only option.

If Bogey had lived long enough, he could have compared the roast beef at the Ritz to the steak and lobster at the ball park. Bogey doesn't strike me as the type who would choose to watch a baseball game in a four star air conditioned restaurant environment.

I'm also not that type, but for those who are, most ballparks can accommodate that desire. If your ticket is in a suite or you plan to watch from an indoor restaurant, remember to dress for an indoor venue and not an outdoor venue.

For the rest of us, ballparks have concession stands, many, many concession stands. The thing is that the concession stands don't all carry the same fare. It's easy to go to a concession stand, look at the menu board and choose. But if you do it that way, you could miss out on a better option at a different stand.

In the previous chapter, I mentioned that a program could help you find the right concession

The Only Thing Cheap is the Seat

stand for your culinary delight, but if you don't have a program, you can still walk around and see what's available. If you're the hot dog and popcorn type, you'll find what you want easily, but don't presume those are your only choices.

By the way, just as different food stands offer different fare, different libation stands offer different brews. If you don't find your favorite beverage at the first stand you visit, ask or walk around a bit. There's a good chance that a different concession stand will have it.

Another diversion offered at most ballparks is activities for children. If you have children, they are likely to find these without you even looking for them. These games aren't usually cheap, but they are an experience that children tend to enjoy at least as much if not more than the game itself. If you don't have children, I still recommend visiting them occasionally. Nothing rekindles the childhood joy of the baseball experience like watching children enjoy it.

Lastly, no trip to the ballpark is complete without a trip to the gift shop. More accurately, it's not complete without a trip to one or more of the many gift shops. Gift shops have also changed for the better recently. One thing that's great about them now is that there is truly something for everybody.

Thanks to Alyssa Milano's line of baseball apparel for women, and more recently, Victoria's Secret's partnership with Major League Baseball, gift shops not only have something for women, they have stylish apparel for women. This is a vast improvement over the days, when the women's aisle in the gift shop consisted of replica tee shirts that looked exactly like the men's shirts except that they came in smaller sizes and the numbers were pink.

Additionally, gift shops now often carry products related to other baseball teams, as well as other local sports teams. Plus, some offer trinkets, such as pencils and keychains, that won't break the budget for most fans.

Don't Be That Dude

"We don't devote enough scientific research to finding a cure for jerks."
— Bill Watterson

I don't think I have to specify who 'that dude' is in the title of the chapter. Anybody who's attended public events even a few times, has had the displeasure of sitting too close to that dude that nobody wants to sit near. For the purpose of this section, 'dude' is not demographically specific. In my experience, 'that dude' can be young or old, male or female, etc.

Sometimes, 'those dudes' are trying to be like that, either because they are basically bad people or because they think it's the only way to impress their buddies. Come to think of it, those may actually be the same reason.

This chapter isn't written for them. The only way to help those people would be to have ushers and security remove them from the stadium. Unfortunately, 'that dude,' also spends money on concessions (often more money than the average fan, since beer is one of the more expensive concessions), so in some stadiums, security is reluctant to remove paying customers, even obnoxious ones. If you end up in that situation, the next chapter on seat surfing might be helpful.

This chapter is for the perfectly nice person, who doesn't want to be that dude. The thing is, as hard as it is to admit, we all run the risk of being that dude on accident, sometimes. We've all done it. I have a theory that every time I hear the phrase 'excuse me,' it means that at that moment I need to consider if I accidentally became that dude in that situation. That's probably too high a standard to expect everybody to accept, especially at a baseball game, but that's the baseline I had in mind when I decided to write this section.

As it applies to a baseball game, the objective of anybody not wanting to be 'that dude' should be to avoid as much as possible preventing other fans from seeing and enjoying the game. That sounds simple, but the fact is that it is not always possible. At some point, every fan at the game is going to end up blocking somebody's view. The best we can do is minimize these times.

To do that, take advantage of game breaks as much as possible. If you can, try to leave your seat and return to your seat between innings, instead of during the game. You can usually wait with the ushers at the entrance to wait for a half inning to end, and still see the game. At hockey games, in the lower sections, they actually require this for safety reasons. Even though baseballs fly into the crowd way more often than hockey pucks, most baseball stadiums don't yet have this rule. Until they do, you should still follow it, if you don't want to be 'that dude.'

Having said that, I also know that you can't always avoid leaving or getting to your seat during the game. When you have to leave your seat during a game, here are a few basics. Don't dawdle; have your things in order before you stand up and walk out as quickly as possible, while making sure you give people enough time

The Only Thing Cheap is the Seat

to move their food, drinks and knees out of the pathway.

Generally, you should walk toward the aisle that requires passing the least number people. However, if you are near the middle of the row and the people on one side are your friends, it's sometimes better to leave that way. Your friends shouldn't mind making way for you to leave. Also, remember that unless you're in the last row, any time you stand up, wherever you stand up, you're probably blocking somebody's view of the game. Don't stand in the aisle to buy your popcorn or beer. Don't stand in the aisle even if you run into your oldest friend. If you feel you have to catch up on old times, find an empty seat and sit down. If there are no empty seats, go out to the concourse to chat.

On the subject of being in the way, my next piece of advice regarding not being 'that dude' is about the wave. Most serious baseball fans will tell you that the wave has no place in the game. I might tell you the same thing, but I know it doesn't matter. Instead, I'll simply make a few suggestions on wave etiquette.

- Never attempt to start or continue a wave while your team is in the field. Some people say you should never start a wave while your team is at bat (and I agree with them). However, if a wave has any impact on the game as a distraction it is nine times more likely to affect one of the nine players in the field as it is to affect the one player at the plate.

- If you try to start a wave three times without success, give it up. Most fans know what a wave is by now. If nobody's interested, move on. There are plenty of ways to have fun at a ballpark without starting the wave.

- If you think you've started a wave and another section stops it, don't boo; don't even get mad. A wave is only of value, if it ever is, if the entire stadium is into it.

- If you do get a wave started, or decide to keep one going, remember to sit down as soon as it moves to the next section. This is not only common courtesy; it's also an important aspect of the wave. If people are standing when the wave reaches their sections, it's not a wave. It's just a bunch of people standing up for no good reason.

Having covered the most clearly defined aspects of not being 'that dude,' I'll finish with the one that I must admit is kind of a gray area. That is the rule/guideline about only standing up during key moments of the game. It's a gray area because everybody has a different definition of what is a key moment of the game. The top the of ninth with two outs and two strikes in a close game is clearly a key moment. Generally, the crowd rises in unison, and begins to clap and chant. This is the type of moment that makes baseball America's game.

But most baseball games have other moments that inspire the same emotion in some of the fans, but not all. For instance, a rookie pitcher makes his Major League debut, and has made it into the fifth inning with two outs. If the kid gets one more out, he'll have the chance to win in his first start. Those fans who have been tracking him since the day the team drafted him have an emotional investment in this moment.

The casual fan behind that fan isn't wrong for wondering why the person in front of him is acting like it's the ninth inning of game seven of the World Series, but the fan who is standing and cheering has every right to do so. My suggestion is to stand for the key moment, and then at a break in the game later, politely explain to the fans behind you why the moment was so special to you. Not only does this ease hard feelings, I've also found that it sometimes turns casual fans into rabid fans.

One should not, however, pick random moments of the game to stand up. Don't stand

The Only Thing Cheap is the Seat

up for an opposing player's every at-bat, for instance, just because you have him on your fantasy team. Don't stand up after every base hit, expecting to start a standing ovation. I will close this chapter with two more absolutes of being a decent person at a baseball game.

One, unless you are at Wrigley Field, never boo a fan who catches a home run ball and chooses not to throw it back. It's a cute, if somewhat stupid, tradition for the lovable Cubbies, but it makes no sense. When a fan throws a ball back, he or she loses a souvenir, a ball boy or ball girl retrieves it and gives it to a fan in a more expensive seat, and the run(s) still count. If a fan wants to throw it back, I have little problem with that, but do not boo those who are smart enough to know better.

Two, and this should go without saying, but sadly it does not. Never, ever stand up while the game is in play so you and your friend in another section can wave at each other.

The Fine Art of Heckling

"What is both surprising and delightful is that spectators are allowed, and even expected, to join in the vocal part of the game."

- George Bernard Shaw

The Only Thing Cheap is the Seat

An astute reader might have noted that I did not include heckling in the chapter on how not to be 'that dude.' The reason for this is simple. Heckling, in and of itself, doesn't make you 'that dude.' Heckling, if you are 'that dude,' lets everybody know that you are, but many people heckle players without being 'that dude.'

Obviously, anything you yell at a player that is blatantly offensive makes you 'that dude,' but the act of yelling at a player doesn't automatically make you 'that dude.' If you want to yell at the players, go for it. Just don't yell anything you wouldn't want somebody to yell at your mother or your child, and you should be staying on the not 'that dude' side of the fence.

Professional athletes don't usually enjoy heckling, but for the most part they accept it as part of the working conditions they accepted when they chose to play a game for money. Obviously, attacks on a player's personal life are always out of line. However, most players have stories about being entertained by comments from fans that were both original and amusing. I'd share some examples, but if I did and you tried to use one, it would no longer be original, and therefore, probably not amusing.

Instead, I'll share two examples that I personally witnessed at Texas Rangers' games. The first occurred in 1973 at the old Turnpike Stadium. The light hitting shortstop, Jim Mason, was in (as he often was) a bit of slump. Never a great hitter, he was currently struggling to make contact at all. After he had swung at and missed two pitches, a fan in the first row on the third base side yelled, "It's the little white thing, Jim!"

On the next pitch, Jim Mason hit one of the three home runs he would hit that year, and one of the twelve he would hit in his nine year major league career. As he rounded third base, he pumped his fist and pointed at the fan while wearing a smile that would have made the Cheshire cat proud.

The second example occurred in 1999 at the stadium currently known as Rangers Ballpark in

The Only Thing Cheap is the Seat

Arlington. The stadium probably had a sponsor at that time, but I'm not interested in promoting that company now. This example involves slick-fielding shortstop Royce Clayton (a former all-star still in the prime of his career).

For five innings, the Rangers' opponent pounded the hole between the third baseman and the shortstop (known in baseball parlance as the 5.5 hole). Every hit was a true hit, neither the third baseman, nor Royce Clayton ever had a chance to stop one of the hits, but it was frustrating for the fans to watch. After, one too many hits, and perhaps one too many beers, a heckler behind the third base dugout, who would go on to write this book, yelled, "Hey Royce, it wouldn't hurt you to lay out for one of those!"

A few pitches later, another ball went into the 5.5 hole. Clayton took two quick steps, dove into the hole and missed the ball by far enough that it was clear that no slick fielding infielder in his position would normally have bothered to dive. It was the kind of dive his teammates would likely call showboating. Clayton stood up, put his right hand on his hamstring and limped to the outfield for the cutoff throw.

The inning ended without incident, and Clayton jogged toward the dugout with his hand again on his hamstring. As he got to the warning track, he took his hand off his hamstring, pointed toward where the heckler was sitting, and said, "Gotcha!" I'm pretty sure his teammates had no problem with the dive.

These are just two examples of players having fun with hecklers. The main take away from this is the players will more likely have fun with a heckler if the heckler is not making personal attacks or saying offensive things. In both of the above examples, the heckling was no different, or if different, much tamer, than what the players hear from teammates on a daily basis. If you heckle within the framework of good sportsmanship, the sportsmen who play the game, will likely respond in kind. If you don't, they won't. It's as simple as that.

Seat Surfing

"I have discovered in twenty years of moving around a ball park, that the knowledge of the game is usually in inverse proportion to the price of the seats."

— Bill Veeck

Seat surfing, as defined in this book, is the art of moving to a seat in a stadium other than the one for which one owns a ticket. Obviously, this is not an activity that is sanctioned by Major League Baseball. It is, however, as much a part of the game as brushback pitches, stolen signs and heckling.

My publisher's legal team insists that I mention that nothing in this chapter or this book is meant to convey the idea that I, or the publisher, condone in any way the horrible, despicable, dishonest act of seat surfing. Now, that the legal team is satisfied, I'll continue.

A man once suggested to me that life in a civilized society comes with two types of statutes: rules and guidelines. Rules, he opined, are those statutes that should always be obeyed, such as not stealing a car or breaking into a house.

Guidelines were his term for things like speed limits and the number of items in your basket at the grocery store that should be regarded as flexible starting points, not absolute certainties. I'm not sure if I ever believed his theory in general, but it does seem to apply quite accurately to this topic.

The rule is that every customer gets a ticket and is supposed to sit in the seat assigned, or if the ticket is standing room only, not sit in a seat. That is most definitely the rule. That rule, however, is universally treated as a guideline in most ballparks. Fans are not encouraged to seat surf, but usually are not discouraged either. To me, that makes it a guideline.

So, the statute about where to sit, is a guideline, but if you want to do it, it's a good idea to follow what I used to call the 'unwritten rules of seat surfing.' Obviously, I can't call them that, anymore, since they have now become written rules. So from this point forward, I'll call them the:

<u>Rules For Not Accepting Seating Guidelines</u>.

To paraphrase a line from Cameron Crow's classic film, "Fast Times at Ridgemont High":

Learn them. Know them. Live them.

- Never try to defend your right to be in a seat that isn't yours. If you are asked to move, move politely without fuss. Some of this was covered in an earlier chapter. You can't argue about who's seat it is without being 'that dude.' You also can't win that argument, so why bother.
- Never risk serious injury getting to or from a seat that isn't yours. Jumping over rails to get to a different seat is a good way to call attention to the fact that you're seat surfing. Doing so to get away after being caught is an overreaction with a real possibility of unacceptably severe consequences. Repeat after me, '**It is not worth it.**'
- Never argue with an usher. The usher is there to improve the fans' experience. The

The Only Thing Cheap is the Seat

ushers receive paychecks from management with the understanding that the usher will help the fans enjoy the game. If you run afoul of an usher, you are always in the wrong. (Also, security personnel, are paid in large part to keep an eye on the ushers, and will never side against one). Arguing with an usher or a ballpark security guard is like arguing with a bouncer. Even if you happen to be correct, you aren't likely to win, so don't. Plus, in both cases, there is almost no chance that you are correct.

- Always respect your fellow fans. All seat surfing activity should be conducted with maximum effort to ensure that you don't lessen even one other fan's enjoyment of the game.
- Never move to a premium seat prior to the bottom of the third inning. There's nothing wrong with scouting out the seat you may want to borrow sooner, but traffic and other issues often make it hard for real fans with

premium seats to get to the game on time. The end of the third inning is the absolute earliest that a seat surfer should start moving toward one of those seats.

- Don't plan to spend the entire night in a surfed seat. There's a reason it's called seat surfing, not seat camping.

Those are the 'Rules For Not Accepting Seating Guidelines.' As mentioned earlier, all seat surfers should learn them, know them, live them. But the great thing about seat surfing is that if you do it right, none of the rules are likely to detract from the experience.

The first thing to know is that seat surfing isn't just about trying to sit in a more expensive seat than you can afford, it's about maximizing the ballpark experience no matter where your ticket says you should be sitting. Now that you have read the rules, and have learned them, know them, and have promised that you'll live them, let's surf. Getting closer to the field in a more expensive seat is one reason to seat surf, but it isn't the only reason. I don't even think it's the best reason. Here are four of my favorites:

- Arguably, the best reason to seat surf is to get away from 'that dude.' If you're stuck by a dude or group of dudes that are ruining your enjoyment of the game, go surfing. As discussed earlier, you can ask security or an usher to do something about 'that dude,' but that doesn't always work. Seat surfing almost always does.
- Another good reason for surfing is to get out of the heat. Many people surf to a higher seat to get to a shaded spot or a spot with a better breeze.
- Similarly, some people surf to get out of the rain. This surfing is so popular that the covered areas may get really crowded if it rains for some time without the game being halted.

- Seat surfing is also a good way to get to know the stadium so you can decide where you'd like to buy tickets to future games. As discussed in an earlier chapter, many factors are in play when choosing where to buy a ticket. Actually, sitting in that seat for a few innings provides one with a great opportunity to evaluate them.

Those four reasons for seat surfing are my favorites, but they are also popular with another group of people. I mentioned earlier that most ushers and ballpark employees consider themselves to be in the customer service business, not the statute and guideline enforcement business.

A few, however, view their positions in reverse, but in my experience, each of the four reasons listed above, often have a magically calming effect on those few who actually take a hard line stance regarding seat surfing. I would never suggest that one should lie about why one is in a seat, but I would suggest that if confronted, it would be a good idea to use one or more of the above four explanations, if possible.

I also realize that some readers are not interested in seat surfing 'laterally' for any reason, and are expecting this chapter to teach them how to get down on the front row behind home plate for the price of their eight dollar ticket in the nosebleed section. Not wishing to disappoint even a single reader, here goes:

- Make sure you are fully versed on the <u>Rules For Not Accepting Seating Guidelines</u>, and ready to live them.
- Scout out the section into which you are hoping to surf. Make sure there are empty seats and make sure the usher isn't checking every ticket.
- Gather everything that you will want to have when you find a seat. Never surf to a seat, and then decide you need to go buy popcorn or a beer to celebrate.

- Make your move between innings or during a pitching change. Not only does this keep you from being 'that dude,' it also makes it easier. More people are moving around, so it is easier to blend into the flow.
- Decide on your seat before you enter the section and walk straight to it and sit down. You should walk to what you've decided will now be your seat as closely as possible to the way a school principal walks through the halls of the school. There should be no uncertainty in your stride.
- If the usher asks to see your ticket, smile engagingly, point indirectly toward the seats you've chosen, and say something along the lines of, "Thanks, I know where to go." If she insists on seeing the ticket, just let it go, return to the concourse and scout out a different section.

- Do not draw attention to yourself. If being in this seat is a ~~Kodak Moment~~… err…a Facebook or Instagram photo op for you, at least wait until you've settled in before taking the pictures. Nothing screams 'seat surfer' louder than taking pictures before even getting settled.

Baseball Reindeer Games

"Look Pee Wee. I think he's kissing her on the strikes, and she's kissing him on the balls."
— Dizzy Dean (Probably Not)

There is no evidence that I can find that proves definitively that Dizzy Dean and Pee Wee Reese did not ever observe a couple enjoying a few kisses in the crowd at a baseball game, and have a conversation which concluded with the preceding hilarious quotation. However, it probably didn't happen. Even if it did happen, it wouldn't be the subject of this chapter.

Feel free to kiss your date at a baseball game whenever you both so desire. Especially feel free to do so when the in-stadium scoreboard suggests that you do so in a between innings "Kiss Cam" bit. The only caveat is that you make sure you don't become 'that guy' or 'that girl' by turning a romantic moment into an over the top public display of affection that will bother other fans and probably get you both removed from the stadium.

For the purpose of this chapter, "Reindeer Games" will not be defined (as it is in Urban Dictionary's Definition 6) as a code name for sex. Instead, the original version from Rudolf will apply: games that are only enjoyed by certain groups. Unlike those reindeer who excluded poor Rudolf, this chapter is being written so all the Rudolfs can join us in our baseball reindeer games.

As discussed earlier, one of the most popular baseball games is the wave. Properly done, it can be a fun diversion during a game that is not entertaining the crowd. As long as it doesn't hurt the home team, or interfere with the fans' ability to take in a crucial moment of the game, it can be a fun game.

Many other games can be played at the ballpark without any risk of impact on other fans. Sometimes, the team provides them or they are provided with your program in the form of a bingo card. These bingo cards are not filled with letter-number combinations like B2 or F4, but instead have play combinations like 6-4-3 (double play ground out, shortstop to second base to first base) or F-7 (Fly out to left field).

The Only Thing Cheap is the Seat

To win, you have to win like any other bingo game by completing a row, but at the ballpark it's not that easy. You can't just yell "Bingo" and collect a prize. You have to present your winning card at a designated place. If you decide to play a bingo card, and are close to a win, you should try to seat surf near that designated place so you can turn in your card as soon as possible.

For the record, close to winning doesn't simply mean having four in a row needing only the fifth play. If the fifth play is a triple play started by the right fielder (TP 9-6-2), or a double play grounder from first base to third base, (DP 3-5), the odds are stacked tremendously against you winning the game on the next pitch.

Baseball, like almost every other activity, also lends itself to a few drinking games. Obviously, my legal team, and my publisher's legal team insist that I make it clear that I/we don't endorse any of these drinking games. I/we also insist that a designated driver should be securely in place before engaging in a baseball drinking game at the ballpark.

As with all drinking games, all players must be of legal age to participate, and each player should decide what beverage and what quantity of the beverage constitutes a drink. When playing a drinking game at a ballpark, I recommend factoring in the price of the beverages into that decision. With that said, here are a couple of fun drinking games for fans at the ballpark.

Putting in the Call is my favorite, in part because the rules are pretty simple. At any point of the game any player can call for a home run. If the batter so called hits a home run, the other players drink. If the batter makes an out, the player who called it drinks. If the batter reaches base without a home run, the game continues.

Pass the Flask is another fairly simple game. Since most ballparks don't permit flasks of alcohol, any token object can be used instead of the flask. The game starts with one player

The Only Thing Cheap is the Seat

holding the 'flask.' After every at bat, the 'flask' is passed to the next player. When a run scores, the player holding the 'flask' drinks.

Pass the Flask can also be a simple gambling game for those so inclined. Instead of a flask or a token, simply substitute an empty cup. After each at bat, the person holding the cup adds a dollar to the cup before passing it on. The person with the cup when a run scores, gets the money, puts a dollar back in and the game continues. The stakes can be lowered by using coins instead of dollars or only passing the cup after every half inning or inning. The stakes can be raised by using Benjamins instead of dollars or passing the cup after every pitch.

That Doesn't Make Sense

"A foolish consistency is the hobgoblin of simple minds."

— Ralph Waldo Emerson

The Only Thing Cheap is the Seat

Baseball, for the most part, is a logical game. Most of the rules make sense and are uniformly applied. A batted ball which is caught in the air is an out. It's simple, direct and consistent. Any time a batted ball is caught in the air, it's an out.

Baseball has no complicated block or charge calls like basketball. It has no incomprehensible pass interference rules like football. It has no blue lines or red lines or goalie creases like hockey.

In baseball, if you reach a base safely, you're safe. If you reach home plate safely, it's a run; exactly one run, every time. No three point shots, no six point touchdown, no one point or two point conversions, no shootouts. Sure, you can score four runs on a grand slam, but only one run scores at a time.

Granted, there are a few rare exceptions, but generally, when a runner reaches home plate safely, it's one run. No need to look for penalty flags, or review to make sure he didn't step out of bounds like in football. A few times a year a runner might be called out on review because he missed a base, or left a base too soon while tagging up on a fly, but it's very rare for that to happen. Many baseball fans have never, and will never witness anything like that.

For many baseball fans, this consistent simplicity is one of the beauties of the great game. For many non-fans, it is part of the slow pace that causes them to prefer the more action-packed sports. However one feels about it, it is hard to conclude that baseball's consistency is the foolish kind that Emerson so elegantly derided.

It is especially difficult to view it that way in light of the fact that baseball manages in spite of this general consistency, to incorporate three of the silliest rules in all of professional sports. The silliest and most famous of the three is the Infield Fly Rule, which also qualifies as one of the most discussed rules in professional sports

I'll get to that rule shortly, I want to start with the one play in baseball that has long been subject to review. In fact, it's possible that the check swing on a pitch outside of the strike zone is the earliest example of a reviewable call. In practice, it works fairly simply.

The pitch is thrown, the batter starts to swing, decides not to swing and stops his swing. The home plate umpire calls the pitch a ball. As discussed earlier, in most other baseball events, that is the end of the event. Not so much, in this case. If the catcher thinks the batter failed to check his swing, he can appeal the call to a base umpire. When I first started watching baseball, this was usually done, by asking the home plate umpire to check, but lately, that courtesy no longer appears to be required.

Now, the catcher points to the base, the base umpire makes the call, either by taciturnly signaling safe as we discussed in a previous chapter, or emphatically calling a strike and in effect overruling another umpire's call without so much as a short conversation.

Obviously, this is completely at odds with the general rules of officiating in every sport in the world. It is also contrary to the actual rules of Major League Baseball. More specifically, it violates Rule 9.02(a) or the Official MLB rules, which reads as follows:

> Any umpire's decision which involves judgment, such as, but not limited to, whether a batted ball is fair or foul, whether a pitch is a strike or a ball, or whether a runner is safe or out, is final. No player, manager, coach or substitute shall object to any such judgment decisions.

Basically, baseball umpires and the game in general, accept as a matter of course, repeated violations of its own rule. As a fan, this makes no sense to me. As a former umpire, this makes no sense to me and offends my sense of fairness.

The only good thing to spring forth from this unacceptable, accepted custom is the irony and humor that can be derived, every time three-time all-star Adrian Beltre beats the catcher and homeplate umpire to the punch by appealing his own check swing before the umpire has time to make the call.

As far as I know, he's the only major leaguer to engage in this preemptive, 'strike,' doesn't seem the right word, so let's go with preemptive action. Maybe, if more major league hitters would adopt this plan, these constant appeals to the base umpire could finally end.

The second play in baseball that doesn't make any sense also seems simple. Here is rule 6.9(B) which explains it quite clearly:

> The batter becomes a runner when the third strike called by the umpire is not caught, providing (1) first base is unoccupied, or (2) first base is occupied with two out.

That seems simple enough, provided that one understands that by becoming a runner, the batter is promised only the opportunity to run toward first base in the hopes of not being thrown out. The batter also becomes a runner when he hits a fair ball that bounces once and is caught by the pitcher.

Where it begins to not make any sense is when one realizes that very few pitches in the strike zone ever pass the catcher. Most strikes that pass the catcher are swinging strikes, batters swinging at pitches so far out of the strike zone that the catcher has no chance to catch them.

These pitches usually end up at the backstop and the batter usually reaches first base safely. Thus, the batter's team is rewarded for his decision to swing futilely at a pitch he couldn't hit and never should have swung at.

This not only doesn't make any sense, it runs counter to everything modern man believes sporting endeavors should embody. If the people who came up with this rule ran the National Basketball Association, a free throw might be worth one point, while an airball on a free throw attempt would be worth two points. Wilt and

Shaq might like that rule, but it still wouldn't make any sense.

Now, let's look at the Infield Fly Rule, which is fairly easy to apply, but apparently a bit more complicated to define:

> An INFIELD FLY is a fair fly ball (not including a line drive nor an attempted bunt) which can be caught by an infielder with ordinary effort, when first and second, or first, second and third bases are occupied, before two are out. The pitcher, catcher and any outfielder who stations himself in the infield on the play shall be considered infielders for the purpose of this rule.
>
> When it seems apparent that a batted ball will be an Infield Fly, the umpire shall immediately declare "Infield Fly" for the benefit of the runners. If the ball is near the baselines, the umpire shall declare "Infield Fly, if Fair."

The ball is alive and runners may advance at the risk of the ball being caught, or retouch and advance after the ball is touched, the same as on any fly ball. If the hit becomes a foul ball, it is treated the same as any foul.

If a declared Infield Fly is allowed to fall untouched to the ground, and bounces foul before passing first or third base, it is a foul ball. If a declared Infield Fly falls untouched to the ground outside the baseline, and bounces fair before passing first or third base, it is an Infield Fly.

Rule 2.00 (Infield Fly) Comment: On the infield fly rule the umpire is to rule whether the ball could ordinarily have been handled by an infielder, not by some arbitrary limitation such as the grass, or the base lines. The umpire must rule also that a ball is an infield fly, even if handled by an outfielder, if, in the

The Only Thing Cheap is the Seat

umpire's judgment, the ball could have been as easily handled by an infielder. The infield fly is in no sense to be considered an appeal play. The umpire's judgment must govern, and the decision should be made immediately.

When an infield fly rule is called, runners may advance at their own risk. If on an infield fly rule, the infielder intentionally drops a fair ball, the ball remains in play despite the provisions of Rule 6.05 (L). The infield fly rule takes precedence.

To paraphrase, the Infield Fly Rule applies with runners on first and second and less than two outs to a fair pop fly that could be easily caught by an infielder. The rule has been a blessing to many an amateur infielder who has missed a pop fly that he should have caught and been rewarded with an out anyway.

It is important to note, however, that the rule is actually meant for the benefit of the baserunners, which explains why the rule includes the phrase "for the benefit of the runners." It is only after a new umpire understands that fact, that he truly learns to correctly apply the rule.

The rule is designed to prevent the defensive team from letting the ball drop and throwing out the lead runners for a possible double play. And that is why the rule doesn't make any sense. Nobody has ever been able to explain to me why the defensive team should not be allowed to turn a poorly hit ball into two outs.

After all, the defense is allowed to get two outs on any other ball. A hard hit ground ball to third can be turned into an around the horn double play. A line drive to first can be turned into an unassisted double play. A strike out on an attempted steal can be turned into a strike 'em out throw 'em out double play. Even a fly ball to the outfield can become a double play. There is no sensible reason why the routine pop fly to the infield is the only batted ball which is exempt from the possibility of a double play.

These rules are entrenched in the game, and are unlikely to ever be changed. They don't make sense, but they are probably here to stay. At least now, when you tell somebody you don't understand the Infield Fly Rule, you won't be admitting that you're not a baseball expert, you'll be bragging about how well you understand the game.

Second Guessing Second Guessers

"Baseball is the only field of endeavor where a man can succeed three times out of ten and be considered a good performer."

— Ted Williams

The Only Thing Cheap is the Seat

The game of baseball lends itself to the joy of second guessing more than any other game. Everything happens at a measured pace that allows time for it. The thing is that just because the game makes it easy, doesn't mean that the second guesser is always right.

There are two major types of second guessers. One type is the know-it-all who only knows to second guess when the play is over and the decision didn't work out. This type tends to boo loudly and it's sometimes hard to tell if he would rather have the team succeed, or have something to complain about.

The second type is the baseball expert who has numbers to back up his opinions. He or she may be an oldtimer who's been watching baseball for 50 years or more. He might also be a youngster who has studied all of the 'advanced metrics' that now permeate the game or somebody who read or saw *Moneyball*, and thinks he knows 'advanced metrics.'

I'll get to *Moneyball* and the 'advanced metrics' people later. This chapter focuses on the art of second guessing. Specifically, it's about why it's so easy to do, and how to do it in an enjoyable, rational way.

The main thing to realize is that baseball is a game based on failure. The most successful players in the game, the ones who are now in the Hall of Fame, failed often throughout their careers.

Ted Williams is arguably the greatest hitter who ever lived. He finished his career with an On Baseball Percentage of 0.482. On base percentage is the number of times he reached base divided by his number of plate appearances.

For Ted Williams, the stat is based on 9,788 plate appearances, with 2,654 hits and 2,021 walks. That means that, in almost 10,000 plate appearance, he failed to get a hit or draw a walk in 52% of those. A little simple math tells us that the great Ted Williams made outs in 5,113 of his

The Only Thing Cheap is the Seat

plate appearances. You may ask what this means to the second guesser.

The answer can be found by putting yourself in the position of your favorite team's manager. Imagine that your team's manager finds himself in a tie game in the bottom of the ninth inning of game seven of the World Series.

Now imagine that due to some fortunate series of events, he suddenly finds that he has Ted Williams, arguably the greatest hitter of all time, healthy, in his prime, on his bench available to pinch hit.

For this discussion, we will dismiss the question of why Ted Williams has been sitting on the bench unused, and just presume he arrived only at this moment. Your manager, if he is smart, will most certainly plan to use Ted Williams as a pinch hitter.

That decision is the easy part. But, baseball is not easy. When do you send this great hitter to pinch hit? Does he lead off, and risk that he might get a hit, but then be stranded by the inferior hitters who follow? Does he wait for somebody to reach the base, and risk the possibility that nobody will reach base?

There is not one right answer to any of these questions, but after the inning ends, the second guessers, will always think they know what the right answer should have been. But let's be optimistic.

Let's say the manager makes a reasonable decision based on his lineup that suggests that one or more of the first three hitters due up have a good chance to get on base. Let's even be optimistic enough to suggest that two of them do, in fact, reach base.

Now, the manager has runners on first and second with one out in a tie game. A base hit could win the game. He looks to his left, and decides to pinch-hit with the greatest hitter the game has ever seen.

It seems logical, and the home crowd will stand and applaud as he walks to the plate anticipating that the greatest hitter in the game

The Only Thing Cheap is the Seat

will deliver a heroic game winning hit. The crowd stays standing as he approaches the plate.

But what happens when the other team's manager walks to the mound and instructs the pitcher to walk him intentionally? The fans boo as the walk is issued. Then they boo even louder as the next hitter grounds into a double play.

Then somebody in the crowd, probably many of the people in the crowd, turns to his buddy and says loudly, "Why did that stupid manager send the best hitter in the history of the game to the plate just to let him be walked intentionally?"

Was the manager wrong? Are the second guessers right? The answer to both of these questions is Yes and No. Baseball is a game of failure. The manager's decision was reasonable. The second guesser's disappointment is valid.

But to make my point on second guessing more vivid, let's get even more optimistic. Let's pretend that our favorite team managed to get the bases loaded with two outs in the bottom of the ninth inning of game seven of the World Series. Suddenly, Ted Williams, the greatest hitter of all time, appears in his prime ready to pinch hit.

The manager very wisely makes the decision to use him as a pinch hitter. The crowd stands and applauds as he approaches the plate. The opposing manager has no choice but to pitch to him. The assembled media prepare their stories for their various blogs, websites, news outlets of all kinds.

The excitement is palpable. The atmosphere is electric. The television audience is also standing. The announcer quits reading commercials and waits for his opportunity to be the voice of a moment that will live forever in the history of the game.

And there is a 52% chance that Ted Williams will make an out, and the game will move onto the tenth inning. Baseball is a game of failure.

The Only Thing Cheap is the Seat

That is what makes second guessing so easy, and also what makes managing a temporary job. The internet is full of lists of the greatest managers of all time. The lists span all eras, but the one common link is that almost every manager on every one of them has been fired more than once.

That proves that owners share the fans love of second guessing. It also proves that second guessing doesn't make you right; it just makes you second.

For the record, Ted Williams, arguably the greatest hitter of all time, went on to a career as a Major League Manager. In four seasons, he compiled a record of 273 wins and 364 losses for a winning percentage of 0.429. His team never finished higher than fourth place. As I said, baseball is a game of failure.

Money Bull

"The playoffs are a crapshoot."

— Billy Beane

The Only Thing Cheap is the Seat

Thanks to a book by Michael Lewis and a movie starring Brad Pitt, almost every baseball fan and many people who don't follow baseball know the story of general manager, Billy Beane and his Oakland Athletics. It's been presented as a heartwarming story of a little guy succeeding in the face of seemingly insurmountable odds.

The movie was good. It proved once again that Brad Pitt is a fantastic actor, and not just a Hollywood pretty boy. It also gave Jonah Hill the chance to demonstrate some acting chops that few people even knew he had.

The only thing wrong with the movie, the book or the story is that it's basic premise is fundamentally incorrect on two major issues. The Oakland Athletics are not a small market team, and they have not succeeded because of Billy Beane's *Moneyball* tactics.

We'll start with the question of success. Billy Beane became general manager of the Athletics in 1997. In the fifteen years he's been making the decisions, his teams have been to the playoffs six times. In those years, they have managed to win one playoff series. In the one year that they won a series, they were promptly swept four games to zero in the second round.

We started this chapter with Billy Beane's famous quote in which he expresses his belief that only the regular season can be influenced. He suggests that in a five or seven game playoff, the whims of chance are more important than the quality of the teams on the field.

In the classic comic *Scroogie*, former Phillie Tug McGraw suggested that a playoff series was like a coin flip in that if one team is in over its head, it is likely to get its tail kicked. The real truth is likely somewhere indefinably between these two mindsets, but some things are quite definitive.

One of those definite points is that in the ten years before Billie Beane was named general manager of the Athletics, Oakland went to the playoffs four times and won four playoff series on their way to one World Series title and two

American League pennants. It's safe to presume that nobody in Oakland's front office at that time considered the playoffs to be a crapshoot.

Another point that is easily defined is the concept of a small market team. A small market team is, obviously and redundantly, a team that plays in a small market. Oakland, California is not a small market. No matter how the movie may portray it, no reasonable definition of small market can include Oakland.

Market size lists use similar, but slightly different, metrics based on what media they are serving, but the Oakland/San Francisco area is almost invariably rated between fourth and seventh in terms of market size. Admittedly, there are two baseball teams in that market, but there are two teams in other large markets, as well.

Nobody ever suggests that the Chicago Cubs or White Sox, the Los Angeles Dodgers or Angels, or the New York Yankees or Mets are playing in a small market. To the contrary, those teams are more often accused of having an unfair market size advantage.

Furthermore, sharing the market with another team hasn't kept Oakland's cross town counterpart from being competitive even in the playoffs. As the Giants celebrated their World Series victories in 2010 and 2012, it's safe to presume nobody in their front office suggested that the playoffs are a crapshoot.

It's extremely possible that making a movie about Billy Beane's Oakland A's was redundant. I submit that the movie was already made in 1989 and was called 'Major League.' Like the fictional owner in that comedy, it is apparent that the Oakland owner wants to move his team to a new city.

He seems to believe the best way to make that happen is to get rid of the superstars and bring in '*Moneyball'* type players like Scott Hattieburg. Hattieburg's greatest skill is his ability to get on base, even though he doesn't hit well. To put it another way, he draws walks frequently. The problem is that contrary to what little league coaches have been shouting at their less talented batters for decades, a walk is not as good as a hit. A walk isn't as good as a hit in the little leagues, and it isn't as good as a hit in the Major Leagues. It never has been. If anybody doubts this, ask yourself how many times a manager has ever ordered his pitcher to issue an intentional hit.

As *Moneyball* makes clear, Hattieburg and his walks did contribute to the team's success according to the 'Advanced Metrics' that Beane uses. I submit, though, that his most important contribution to the objective of A's ownership is that not a single fan bought a ticket specifically to see him or any of the other 'Moneyball' players that have graced the team's roster for the last fifteen years.

Advanced Metrics in Quotes

"There are three types of lies -- lies, damn lies, and statistics."

— Benjamin Disraeli (Maybe)

The Only Thing Cheap is the Seat

In part because of *Moneyball*, much more due to the efforts of Bill James and countless other mathematical geniuses, the great game of baseball now has an entire legion of fans who believe the game can be understood only through the use of 'advanced metrics.'

This may be a surprise to some, but I actually love 'advanced metrics.' If I were the General Manager of a team, I would use every available 'advanced metric' to evaluate talent, including coaching talent that I could find.

I write this chapter not to start a debate with the 'advanced metrics' crowd. I also do not write this chapter as an introduction to an 'advanced metrics' course. This chapter is designed to help the casual fan grasp the brilliant, but in some ways, flawed logic which can be found in this new science. My hope is that the casual fan can learn to appreciate the 'advance metrics' without being overwhelmed or intimidated by them.

The definition of 'advanced metrics' depends on the person defining the phrase. Some include statistics most fans understand such as OPS (on base percentage + slugging percentage) .

Others believe that 'advanced metrics' only include statistics that require a calculator, a slide rule, an MBA in statistics and 317.25 interns to compute, such as xFIP (Fielding Independent Pitching). If you have enough interns to do this, here's the formula:

xFIP=((13*(FB% * League-average HR/FB rate)) + (3*(BB+HBP-IBB))-(2*K))/IP + 3.2.

By the way, the above formula is not universally accepted. It can vary from website to website. It also varies from year to year on some websites. It's definitely an 'advanced metric.'

But, the question is, "Does it, or any other 'advanced metric,' mean that the second guesser who uses these metrics is correct about their second guess?" I love a question with a clear and concise answer. The answer to this question is "No."

'Advanced metrics' are fabulous tools for comparing players from different eras or different

The Only Thing Cheap is the Seat

leagues. However, when using them to second guess a player, manager or general manager, one is misapplying a great tool to prove a point for which the tool absolutely does not apply.

In 1983, Toby Harrah said, "Baseball statistics are like a girl in a bikini. They show a lot, but not everything." In the three decades since he made this statement, bikinis and baseball statistics have both changed dramatically, for better or for worse. Both show much more now than they did in 1983, but what he said then, is still 100% true today.

By the way, Toby Harrah is uniquely qualified to talk about statistics, particularly defensive statistics, because in 1976, he became the first and only player in the history of Major League Baseball to play an entire doubleheader at shortstop without recording an assist, a putout or an error defensively. That means he played eighteen innings at the busiest position on the diamond without statistically being involved in even one play.

Numbers and statistics, basic ones like batting average or 'advanced metrics' like xFIP are great for comparison, but they are not baseball. Baseball is both a mental game and an emotional game. No metrics 'advanced' or otherwise can evaluate all of those aspects.

One example is diving into first base. The 'advanced metrics' people say a player should never do that. They say that because they don't understand the true objective. I watched a thirty minute program on television once dedicated to determining if diving into first or running through the base would get a player to the base fastest.

The show was fascinating. It used all the latest video and chronological technology. It showed multiple people running through the base. It showed multiple people diving into first base. It showed all of these people over and over.

It was, in short, a great bit of video for the entertainment of baseball fans of all types. After all the video and all the technology had been shown off and evaluated, the show reached a conclusion on the subject.

I would tell you what it concluded, but there's no need. The question the show sought to answer is completely irrelevant to the game of baseball. A baserunner hustling down the basepath is not doing so with the objective of getting there fastest.

Those who wish to compete for speed have many events in the Track and Field arena in which to compete. In baseball, the goal is not to be fast, the goal is to be safe. That's all that matters in the game of baseball. You may be asking if the two goals aren't related. They are related, but they are not exactly the same thing.

When a baserunner dives into first, he makes it harder, if not impossible for the first baseman to get him out with a tag if the throw pulls him off the base. I was taught, many years ago, to watch the first baseman's feet to see if they were moving in a way that indicates that the throw is offline.

In the Major Leagues, the throws are much faster and much less likely to be offline, so that tactic is less useful. But it is definitely one advantage to be gained by diving into first base.

Another point to consider is that being safe means that as the play unfolds, the umpire calls you safe. Nothing else matters. Instant replay may one day change how the call is made. But that won't change the fact that the call is the event.

I'm not stating that Major League umpires are more likely to miss a call in the runner's favor because he dives. Nor, am I stating that a Major League umpire is less likely to miss a call in the fielder's favor because the runner dives.

I am, however, suggesting that before the second guessers state as fact that diving into first base is a mistake, much more research should be done. We need, for example, to study the tendencies of umpires regarding safe or out calls based on runners who dive and runners

The Only Thing Cheap is the Seat

who run through the base. It would also help to know the exact frequency of offline throws.

Again, I'm not saying that diving into first is a good idea. I'm simply saying that if you are going to second guess professional players, managers and coaches based on your 'advanced metrics,' you should make sure your 'advanced metrics' relate to the actual objective.

Another example of the 'advanced metrics' people missing the objective is the sacrifice bunt. Most 'advanced metrics' suggest that the sacrifice bunt is almost always a bad managerial move. However, every manager in the league continues to call for sacrifice bunts in situations where 'advanced metrics' suggest it is not a good idea.

Are these managers stupid, or do the 'advanced metrics' lie? The answer is neither. The sacrifice bunt does not statistically lead to more total runs for the team that executes it.

That fact leads to a critical mistake that fans of 'advanced metrics' make. They get so caught up in their numbers, that they forget the objective of the team.

The goal is to win enough games to get to the playoffs, then win enough games in the playoffs to make the World Series, then win four games in the World Series.

Most 'advanced metrics' people agree that a tie game in the ninth inning with one on and nobody out and the leadoff hitter batting is one of the rare occasions when the sacrifice bunt is appropriate. That situation is one that might occur in any game, even game seven of the World Series.

It could occur in any game, but it doesn't. In fact, it's pretty rare. How sad would it be if a team reached that point in game seven, but couldn't use the sacrifice bunt, because the leadoff hitter had never bunted in any situation all year long?

That question is rhetorical. The reason it's rhetorical is because all Major League managers know the objective. Not one would ever get

The Only Thing Cheap is the Seat

caught up in 'advanced metrics' enough to allow that to happen. The second guessers have their audience of everybody sitting close enough to them at the game to hear them. Some of them also have blogs and websites where they can complain.

Fortunately, all managers (and most general managers) know better than to listen to them. I hope after you read this, that you will also know better. A baseball season is a marathon, not a sprint.

Even if you go to only one game a year, and even if your team loses that game based on a decision that the guy next to you says 'advanced metrics' helped him 'know' was the wrong call, don't panic. The management team of even the worst team in the game knows more about the game of baseball than 'that dude' sitting next to you does.

The Walk Off

"Hello, Win Column."

— Mark Holtz

The Only Thing Cheap is the Seat

Some say that the home run is the most exciting play in baseball. I don't believe that, but it is the most exalted play. Throughout history, baseball announcers have tried to perfect the call of the home run. Here are a few of the more popular attempts.

- Back, back, back, back, Gone!
- Tell it goodbye
- Kiss it goodbye
- Holy Cow
- Goodbye, baseball
- That ball is history
- Long Gone

All of these are great signature calls for an ordinary home run, but some home runs are special. Two that come to mind are Bobby Thompson's pennant winning home run in the 1951 playoff game against the Dodgers and Kirk Gibson's game winning home run in game one of the 1988 World Series against the Athletics.

Thompson's home run in 1951, became known as the "shot heard round the world," but that happened after the fact. The announcer's call was much more succinct and moving:

> There's a long drive!
> That's gonna be it, I believe!
> The Giants win the pennant!...

Kirk Gibson's home run didn't clinch a pennant. It merely won game one of the World Series. But the win did help the Dodgers win the series, and it was memorable, among other reasons, because he was injured and barely able to run the bases after his pinch hit home run.

That may explain why Vin Scully called the home run this way: "She is gone." Thompson's pennant winning home run and Gibson's World Series home run were both what are now described as "Walk Off Home Runs."

If either of those classic home runs had been hit recently, instead of the classic calls the announcers blessed us with, we would almost

The Only Thing Cheap is the Seat

certainly be told the home run was a walk off home run. A walk off home run is defined as a home run that ends the game.

A great debate rages amongst some fans as to what game ending plays can acceptably be called 'walk offs.' Some purists claim that only home runs should be so called. Others claim that any play that wins the game in the bottom of the ninth inning or extra innings.

The correct answer is much simpler than any of these guidelines. The last play of every game of any sport can be defined as a walk off. Granted, the walk off kneel down by the quarterback in a football game lacks the excitement of the walk off home run, That, however, doesn't change the fact that right after the quarterback kneels, he stands back up, hands the ball to the official and walks off.

The point isn't that the game winning home run isn't a great moment; it is. It's made more magical by the fact that the home team always bats last, which hasn't always been the case. In basketball, a game winning three pointer is as likely to occur on the road, and send a stunned, silent crowd home in disappointment. The point is that the phrase walk off adds nothing to the excitement.

In fact, because the home team doesn't bat in the bottom of the ninth if the game is already won, home fans can delight in a walk off ground ball to first in the top half of the ninth inning. For those who think nothing can match the upside of the walk off home run, let me offer some alternatives

Let's go to April 21, 1978, in historic Dodger Stadium, aka Chez Ravine. The Dodgers are hosting the Houston Astros. Sure, it's only April, so the stakes aren't quite as high as they were for Bobby Thompson and Kirk Gibson, but the game is one of those games for the ages. The Astros scored three runs in the top of the eight to take the lead. Now, it's the bottom of the ninth inning and the home team trails eight to six.

The Only Thing Cheap is the Seat

The Dodgers have runners on first and second with nobody out, and Ron Cey, aka The Penguin, is at the plate. Admittedly, Ron Cey is not the greatest hitter of all time, like Ted Williams was in our earlier hypothetical, but in 1978, he would go on to make the all-star game for the fifth time. He also already had two hits and a walk in this game.

With Steve Garvey and Dusty Baker scheduled to follow, the 40,000 plus Dodger fans in attendance had reason to be optimistic. Since the phrase Walk Off Homer hadn't yet been coined, they simply hoped for a game winning hit from one of the three once or future all stars scheduled to bat next.

Perhaps, at least one fan, if not more, thought to themselves as they waited nervously, "Just end it now, Penguin." If so, unfortunately for them, they got exactly what they asked for, but not at all what they wanted. With both runners moving, Cey lined out to first baseman, Bob Watson, who threw to shortstop, Roger

Metzger who stepped on second to record the second out, and tagged out the runner from first to end the inning and the game.

I know the 44,000 Dodger faithful who had their hearts broken that evening won't agree with me, but that walk off triple play is far more exciting than a simple home run. Perhaps, they can console themselves with the knowledge that their Dodgers recovered from that game and won the National League pennant.

Okay, but maybe you need your walk offs to be driven by the offense. Fine, but we still don't need a home run or even a hit to make that exciting. Let's go to July 1st, 2012, at Miller Park in Milwaukee. The Brewers are hosting the Arizona Diamondbacks. With the game tied one to one in the bottom of the ninth, leadoff hitter Aramis Ramirez draws a walk.

The speedster dances back to the base safely on eight pickoff attempts, which we know drew boos from over 35,000 Brew Crew faithful. Finally, Ramirez breaks for second with one out.

He slides in safely at second as the throw goes past second base and into centerfield. He sprints to third base as the centerfielder retrieves the ball and throws it in. As the throw skips past third base, Ramirez trots home with the winning run. I doubt if anybody at the game wishes they'd witnessed a walk off home run, instead.

Now for my favorite walk off example of a ninth inning game winning run that scored on something other than a home run, or even a hit, I present what I believe to be the only walk off strikeout in the history of Major League Baseball that the team at bat won. Even if it isn't the only one, it is definitely my personal favorite.

It's September 29, 2010, at Rangers Ballpark in Arlington. The Rangers are hosting the Seattle Mariners. In front of about 20,000 fans, the Rangers have scored four runs in the late innings to tie the game at five to five.

In the bottom of the ninth inning with two outs, Mitch Moreland draws a walk. Nelson Cruz, who already has four walk off hits this year is at the plate. The fans are, to say the least, optimistic. Much to their chagrin, Cruz swings and misses at strike three in the dirt. In a previous chapter, I covered rules that don't make sense. Cruz's strikeout was not the third out because it skipped past the catcher, Guillermo Quiroz.

Cruz hustled toward first base, Moreland hustled toward second as Quiroz chased the ball. Quiroz' throw to first was wild and went past first baseman, Justin Smoak, and into right field. Moreland scored on the play, and the Rangers went on to win the American League Pennant.

That walk off was exciting enough for those of us who were in attendance. I hope this walk off is sufficient for those reading it.

HELLO, WIN COLUMN

www.ingramcontent.com/pod-product-compliance
Lightning Source LLC
Chambersburg PA
CBHW071705040426
42446CB00011B/1926